REAL
TALK

REAL TALK

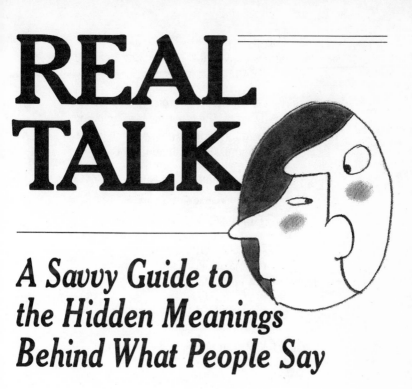

A Savvy Guide to the Hidden Meanings Behind What People Say

BRET INGHAM
Illustrated by **ROY McKIE**

A QUILL INK BOOK
Maxim Publishing Corporation
Fort Lee, N.J.

Library of Congress Catalog Card Number 92-64234

ISBN 0-9624998-1-1 (cl)
ISBN 0-9624998-0-3 (pa)

A Quill Ink Book
Published by Maxim Publishing Corporation
Quill Ink is an imprint of Maxim Publishing Corporation

Queries regarding rights and permissions should be
addressed to:

Quill Ink/Maxim Publishing Corporation
177 Main Street, Suite 367
Fort Lee, NJ 07024

Additional copies of *Real Talk* may be ordered from:
National Book Network
4720 Boston Way
Lanham, MD 20706
1-800-462-6420

Designed by Christine Swirnoff

Printed on acid-free paper

Manufactured in the United States of America

2 4 6 8 10 9 7 5 3 1

*Dedicated to the principle that all
people should be offended equally in
the interest of Real Talk.*

A Real Thanks to: My darling husband, my otherwise super parents whose one quirk is they're "not big on humor books by anybody but Cosby," Lila Holt, the best personal a person could have, Akasha, who can supply enough energy for five books, Margaret Miller, Barbara Dunbar, Jed Eshel, Dia Livingston, Gail Fierstein, ReRe Kirk, Terry Reilly, Rita Frisch, Liz Zalkind, Tom O'Brien, Jack Vartabedian, Mae Castelucci, Rose King, Genie and Bob Birch, Hence Orme, Carol and Cynthia, a dynamite duo, Shirley Stichman, a sensational relative, and to all those at Carm's Cafe where you can always get Real Good Food along with Real Talk.

Also, a real debt of gratitude to some true pros I've been lucky to know: Elliot Tiber, Judith Appelbaum, Marjory Bassett, Michelle Cousin, Catherine Chapin, Maggie Allen, Linda Seger, Joan Brandt, Phyllis Skomorowsky, David Silverman, Frank Curtis, Ginger Wright, Mary Ann Kreger, Florence Janovic, Jeff Yuen, Pat LiBassi, Eric Kampmann, Andrew Osvick, Debra Richman, Suzi Schmittlein, Michelle Shableski, Gail Whitehurst, Judith Stein, Danny Sanchez, Ami Stiver, and last, but most important, to Linda Ripinsky, for not throwing the book at us.

CONTENTS

NOW HEAR THIS

If you were buying a product that came with a "90-Day Guarantee on Parts and Labor," would you realize that's practically a guarantee the machine has been made to fall apart on the 91st day? If your hostess said, "Thanks for stopping by," would you know she was really telling you that it's time to say bye-bye? If you saw a want ad for a job with "No skills required," would you understand that means no one with skills would want the job? If someone said, "I don't want to hurt your feelings but . . . ," would you get the feeling the person was about to do just that? If so, congratulations. You have a knack for Real Talk.

Broadly speaking, there are two kinds of talk: what people say and what people don't say, but do mean. The first is called everything from polite conversation to bull ----, by those who don't care about polite conversation (the typist does). Real Talk is the second.

Few people use Real Talk all the time (try telling a cop what you really think when he gives you a ticket). So, you usually have to translate what you hear. For instance, if a guy trying to seduce you insists he'll "feel the same way in the morning," rest assured what that comes down to is he's always horny after a good night's sleep. When a friend consoles you with, "No, honestly, your hair doesn't look bad cut that way," what she's being honest about is that your only consolation is that your hair will grow back. If a realtor attempts to sell you a house "that's only an hour's commute to the city," you should figure that's at three o'clock in the morning when nobody wants to go there.

I found out how important it is to understand Real Talk at the impressionable age of 13, a time when all I wanted from life was to make the right impression on the class hunk. No small feat, as I was a foot taller than he and had a body that made strangers bet on what it would develop into.

My big shot in the dark, as my mother put it, arrived when I was invited to the "in" crowd's barbecue. I was afraid I would make a fool of myself in front of the cool kids—the hunk was the coolest of the cool. "You've been doing that all year anyway," my brother said encouragingly. A point. And my mother cheered me on, too. "You'll look as good as anyone else there . . . Okay, so maybe you won't look quite as good. That's the beauty of barbecues. It's dark. Who'll see you?"

Because she was anxious to be the first on the block to try a brand new detergent that promised to make clothes smell dreamily clean and, wonder of wonders, eliminate the chore of rinsing out the soap suds, my mother washed everything, from my special training bra to my "in" jeans, with this break-through product. Alas, this was no break for me. A thunderstorm struck at the peak of the party while I was in heaven roasting the hunk's hot dog. My cups—of the training bra—and all of my duds started running over with soap suds. Like the ever-expanding pudding in Woody Allen's movie *Sleeper*, my body seemed to be forever blowing bubbles. A big blob of white trying to disappear into the night, I heard the hunk say, "Look! She's even foaming at the mouth."

I still am. From then on, lucky for you, I've been alert to the soft soap in ads and in everyday chatter as well. This guide to what is truly behind the written and spoken word will keep fast talkers from pulling a fast one on you, help you understand everyone better—from your mother to your lover—and, overall, show you the world as it really is, not as it may seem to the untrained ear.

HOW TO USE THIS MANUAL

Real Talk is best read in small doses—just as you'll hear it in real life. So, for optimum results, take it a chapter at a time or check out the section that most applies to what's important to you at the moment. (For example, it's unlikely you'll be looking for a job and lavishly decorating your home simultaneously. It might pay to dip into the part on making money first.)

CHAPTER ONE ⌣

How to Really Shape Up

Not saying what you mean is par for the course for conversation everywhere from the bedroom to the boardroom—and that's just the b's. Indeed, both places are hotbeds for faking it conversationally, and otherwise. But because Americans firmly believe you have a slimmer chance of making it anywhere if you're not in shape (indeed some women actually pray to be stricken with anorexia, I can vouch for that), dieting seems a fitting spot to begin.

Diet Tip-offs

Pollsters tell us the number one New Year's resolution made in this country is to lose weight—and that's the same one most people break. True dieters are easy to spot. These are the people who expound on the benefits of bran in the system when you want to enjoy your pizza with the works. They talk of clogged arteries on the road to McDonald's. They insist you meet at Jack LaLanne's when you suggest Blimpie Base. They begin to resemble Jack LaLanne while you start to look like a Blimp—well, you get the picture.

And then there are the rest of us. The following statements—whether offered as diet tips or as verbal evidence that one is a member of the sweat set—should be taken with a grain of salt substitute. Or in other words, it's not what comes out of one's mouth about dieting that carries any weight, it's what you put into it.

STATEMENT	REAL TALK
I'm going to start my diet tomorrow.	*I'm going to pig out today.*
If you don't buy junk food, it won't be in the house when you want to eat it.	*It will be in 7-Eleven in the middle of the night, when you want to eat it—the same place you will be.*
I wouldn't be seen eating dessert.	*I eat it where nobody can see me.*

STATEMENT	REAL TALK
Only eat half of what is on your plate.	*That way you can have the rest as a snack.*
Chew slowly.	*And often.*
Go grocery shopping on a full stomach.	*It's a great excuse to eat as much as you want before you go to the store.*
Say no thank you when people offer you food.	*You'll look virtuous and they'll keep offering it until you take it anyway.*
Leave the table as soon as you've finished a meal.	*It's more comfortable to nosh in the living room.*
Use a smaller plate.	*So you get to fill it more frequently.*
Don't use remote control— get up to change the channel on the TV.	*Then you can snatch a snack at the same time.*
Try gargling to pacify your taste buds.	*That will kill the evidence that you just knocked off a pastrami on rye.*

STATEMENT	REAL TALK
Have someone else serve you—instead of helping yourself.	*Then you can't help how much they give you.*
Put your knife and fork down while dining alone.	*You can eat twice as fast with your hands.*
Schedule the times and places you eat.	*So you never miss an opportunity.*

A Dieter's Dictionary: Coming to Real Terms with Losing Weight

The following are key to losing illusions about shedding weight. Hardly inclusive, the list is intended to whet your appetite and help you view being heavy in a new light.

TERM	REAL TALK
Appetite depressant	*Sleep.*
Calorie	*A toxic substance that science has not yet been able to remove from food.*

TERM	REAL TALK
Diets	*A vast variety of food plans all of which forbid the one food you crave at the time you* must *eat it.*
Diet soda	*Ideal beverage to consume with cake, pie, candy, and ice cream when you are cutting down on sweets.*
Doctor's scale	*An instrument that has been doctored to make you weigh more than you did at home.*
Exercise equipment	*Updated medieval torture devices that modern Americans voluntarily take great pains to use.*
Fast food	*High caloric food that you can eat fast on your lunch hour so you have time to go to aerobics class and work off the calories.*

TERM	REAL TALK
Fashion designers	*Largely, fat-phobic individuals dedicated to the principle that women size 14 and above (over a third of American females) should be reduced to wearing polyester.*
Jell-O	*Colorful substance to eat whipped cream from.*
Jogging	*Sport whose chief benefit is that it permits carbohydrate loading.*
Premenstrual syndrome (PMS)	*A premenstrual condition for which the only known medical cure is chocolate.*
Pound	*A measurement of weight that decreases at a much slower rate than it increases.*

TERM	REAL TALK
Size (of clothing)	*That which always happens to run small in the particular style you try on; a perplexing phenomenon giving rise to the expression, "Go figure."*
Tea	*What you have to drink at your aunt's so you can pig out on the pastry.*
Water retention	*Reason you know you gained three pounds overnight when* all *you did was scarf down that many pounds of cheesecake.*
Weight Watchers	*A great place for some people to watch others lose weight.*

Buy the Book: How to Read the Fat Print of a Diet Book

While there's no shortage of how-to-diet books, the supply
has created the need for a guide telling us how to read them.
Here is the lowdown on diet-book lingo for those who have
been taken in as they try to take it off.

CLAIM	REAL TALK
Miraculous Weight Loss Plan!	*The miracle is it doesn't kill you.*
The Diet of the Stars!	*You can't afford it.*
Eat All You Want!	*Throw up the same amount.*
You'll Never Feel Hungry!	*You'll never be thin either.*
A Diet You Can Live With!	*You're going to have to— you lose as fast as a drugged turtle on this one.*
Special Water Diet!	*Your mouth will water for food.*
Easy to Follow Plan!	*You're allowed one food.*

CLAIM	REAL TALK
Permanent Weight Loss Plan!	*This isn't a diet—it's a life sentence.*
Medical Breakthrough Speeds Up Metabolism!	*You'll be on speed—and could have a medical breakdown.*
Alcoholic Beverages Allowed!	*No food.*
Think Yourself Thin!	*Just understand no one else will think you are.*
Pills Kill Your Appetite!	*And replace it with nausea.*
Eat the Food You Love!	*Keep the fat you hate.*
Balanced, Planned Menus for Every Day of the Week!	*You'll never leave the kitchen.*
99% Success Rate at Our Spa!	*As long as clients are confined to the premises for life.*
Last Chance Diet!	*Chances are you won't last on this one either.*
Nibble All You Want Between Meals!	*The same foods rabbits do.*

CLAIM	REAL TALK
Physician's Diet Offered First Time to the Public!	*Physician offered fat book contract.*
The Most Popular Diet Book of the Year!	*It'll be history by next year.*
Change Your Eating Habits with These Potent Pills!	*And your drug habits— we're talking Betty Ford Clinic potential here.*
Helped 1,000 People Lose Weight!	*Has not helped 999 of them keep it off, yo-yo.*

Truth in Food Labeling

To tell the truth, you can't judge a food by its label. For one thing you can't pronounce the words—unless you're super-polysyllabic and pseudoscientific. Can't these people use simpler language? Even the basic info, though, is enough to give you thought for the food. A sampling below:

LABEL	REAL TALK
Contains phenylalanine, potassium benzoate, annato, yucca, calcium silicate, aspartame, sodium nitrate, malic acid, disodium phosphate, ammonium bicarbonate, artificial colors and flavors.	*No room for food.*
This product has been determined to cause cancer in laboratory animals.	*It may in people too. But as it is unethical to test humans, we'll just have to wait and see if you get it.*
Sugar, corn syrup, molasses, and other sweeteners added.	*This product could give cavities to false teeth.*

LABEL	REAL TALK
Lite.	*A miracle of modern labeling, as in lite heavy cream, lite extra thick syrup, lite jumbo dumplings.*
Serving (as in six servings per package).	*An amount derived by testing on laboratory animals the size of mice.*
High in fiber.	*Full of sawdust.*
For best results, keep refrigerated.	*Otherwise, prepare for food poisoning.*
Muffins chock full of blueberries.	*Above the wrapper in the part of the muffin you can see.*
For increased crispiness, heat before serving.	*Product is soggy.*
Product may settle in jar.	*You'll have to settle for less than a jarful.*
No preservatives.	*No shelf life.*

CHAPTER TWO

X-Rated: The Secret Language of Love and Sex

To hear the experts tell it, communication is the answer to many of our relationship problems. But our very terminology on sex and love leaves something to be desired, semantically—not to mention romantically. We speak of one-night stands when much standing probably wasn't going on. Getting to know someone can be more like getting to snow them. And at the end of the line(s), familiarity breeds attempts at still more cover-ups, which accounts for the-wife-is-the-last-to-know syndrome. Hence, a closer look at mouth-to-mouth contact and combat among friends, lovers, spouses, louses (categories may overlap here), strangers, and those we just wish were.

How to Judge a Person Through the Personals

Many of the unattached would love to meet their match. Some even advertise the fact. But if you're going to go public about what you want in private, this is a must read before you proceed. A glance at the personal columns can give the impression that just about everyone available is "good-looking," "well-built," and "sexy." However, an ad in Real Talk might begin, "Bald guy with paunch and occasional impotence who never looks up from TV during sports desires . . ." or "Woman with cellulite who sometimes needs Valium and always forgets to enter amounts in checkbook would like to meet . . ." The following—based upon actual ads and reports from real respondents—aims to answer the question, what's the catch?

PERSONAL AD	REAL TALK
Woman with exotic background seeks man willing to make commitment.	*Illegal alien needs to get admitted to country.*
Made bundle on Wall Street, now looking for discreet woman who wants to tour Alps.	*Insider trader wants female companionship after he taps Swiss bank account.*

PERSONAL AD	REAL TALK
Librarian looking for man who is not dull.	*One of us is enough.*
Desires highly sensual man into healthful living for cozy evenings at home.	*My condom or yours?*
Looking for good-hearted, financially secure man.	*To get me out of debt.*
Free to travel anytime, anywhere.	*Unemployed.*
Looking for a man who has read about the G-spot.	*And will find mine.*
Man with strong libido desires intimate relationship with sexy woman. Quick response. Hurry!	*Horny.*
Stay up to watch sunrise together.	*Lonely insomniac.*
Gray-haired gent desires young chick.	*Impotent, but hoping for comeback.*

PERSONAL AD	REAL TALK
Foreign-born man seeks patient, understanding woman.	*Can't speak English yet.*
Seek sexual relationship with liberated, responsible woman.	*We go dutch on blood tests.*
Motorcyclist seeking off-beat woman into fantasy and play.	*And leather.*
Need someone can confide in.	*Can't afford therapist.*
If you're cautious but open-minded about having an affair, let's talk.	*About whom you've slept with the past 10 years.*
Love to cook.	*Men don't usually like to spring for dinner for me.*
You must be an energetic man who loves children.	*And willing to raise my four.*
Must enjoy long walks.	*Can't afford car.*

PERSONAL AD	REAL TALK
Love lazy Sundays.	*Will sleep over on a Saturday night date.*
Let's cook up a storm: single, male vegetarian loves quiet dinners at home.	*No wok, I walk.*
Italian-American Bronx bachelor still living at home looking for someone down-to-earth to enjoy simple pleasures with.	*So, what do you want to do tonight, Marty?*
M.D. who lived long time in Europe.	*Not smart enough to get in med school in USA.*
Tired of life in fast lane?	*My career is going nowhere.*
Cuddly.	*Okay, chubby.*
Bubbly.	*Okay, a bubble-head.*
Love to play guitar and sing for you.	*Nobody else will listen.*

PERSONAL AD	REAL TALK
Eligible Charles Bronson-type . . . just getting back in circulation.	*Just eligible for parole.*
Photo is extremely important.	*Brains are not.*
Can't get no satisfaction but I'm willing to try with well-endowed man.	*Nonorgasmic to date.*
Digs roses, champagne, gourmet dinners.	*And gold.*
Great smile.	*Teeth capped.*
Ex-businessman, ex-lawyer, ex-teacher (now investor) looking for lasting relationship.	*If you last, you'll be the first thing in my life that has.*
Looking for sexy woman who knows how to please older man who in return will please her with luxuries galore.	*Sugar Daddy who can't score on own looking for hooker.*

PERSONAL AD	REAL TALK
Massively built ex-Marine seeks feminine (NOT feminist) girl, preferably Asian, who loves to give her man massages and breakfast in bed.	*Rambo seeks geisha.*
Let's get together for coffee.	*Brother, can you spare a dime?*
59-year-old bachelor still looking for the right one.	*And, face it, you still will be after meeting me.*
I'm a man who has no vices.	*Except lying.*

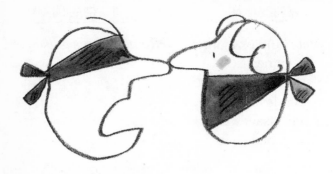

Blind Dates: What to Look Out For

Of course, you don't have to take a chance on the personals when so many of your unhappily married friends go around saying, "You should see the date I have for you. . . ." That's the true part—you *should* see the person first. Still, there's no need to wear blinders just because it's a blind date. The following statements are red lights to stop in the name of what you love and get more data on the date.

STATEMENT	REAL TALK
He can be very persistent if he likes a girl.	*This guy could show up on your doorstep more times than a Jehovah's Witness.*

STATEMENT	REAL TALK
She's older—but she keeps herself up.	*She's had more lifts than a barbell.*
He's on the quiet side.	*He was once taken for dead at a dinner party.*
She *is* on the heavy-set side.	*If you go to a motel, you'll have to ask them to set aside two rooms.*
He has interests other than just football.	*Baseball, basketball—any activity where there are balls.*
Well, she's not a spring chicken.	*You'd need a fire extinguisher to put out the candles on her birthday cake.*
He's a little like Ted Koppel.	*He has the ears—not the brains.*
She's not a yuppie—she has *very* simple tastes.	*This gal thinks 7-Eleven is a gourmet food store.*

STATEMENT	REAL TALK
You could say he's a male chauvinist.	*Let's put it this way: when he dies he'll probably leave his penis to science.*
She's a spiritual person in a modern way.	*She's had to be deprogrammed from three cults.*
I never really noticed exactly how short he is.	*But I did notice he went under—not through—the turnstile at the subway.*
She's a barrel of laughs—I'll tell you that.	*She's shaped like one too—that's what I'm not telling you.*
He's not the three-piece-suit type.	*It wouldn't go with his gold chains, pinky ring, and hoop earrings.*
He's gorgeous—he can have any girl in the office.	*And he has—you'll need an industrial strength condom with this one.*

The (Other) Real Differences Between the Sexes

One reason there's friction—of the wrong kind—between men and women is that they don't speak the same language. This may have given rise to the line, "My wife doesn't understand me." How could she? More important, how can you understand the opposite sex? The following looks at where both sexes are coming from and what happens when they try to come together.

Out of the Mouths of Babes: (What Women Are Really Saying About Men)

WOMAN'S STATEMENT	REAL TALK
It's not that I didn't enjoy the, uh, foreplay.	*It's just I thought it might include something more than putting on your condom.*
There's nothing wrong with premature ejaculation.	*That long-term care at Masters and Johnson can't cure.*

WOMAN'S STATEMENT	REAL TALK
I didn't think I was taking that long.	*I just think a commercial during Monday night football seems short.*
Nobody beats you when it comes to sex, honey.	*You finish first.*
You don't have to know the *exact* location of a woman's clitoris.	*But it would help if you knew the general vicinity and then asked for directions.*
I thought I heard bells.	*But I should have known it was just a false alarm.*
A prenuptial agreement is no way to start a marriage.	*Worse, it's no way to end one.*
It's not surprising so many women have to masturbate to have an orgasm.	*It's just more proof a woman's work is never done.*
My husband never takes sleeping pills.	*He just has sex with me instead.*

WOMAN'S STATEMENT	REAL TALK
It wasn't so bad when my husband fell asleep after sex.	*But now it seems as if he sleeps during it.*

Ah, Men! (What Men Are Really Saying About Women)

Some men open their mouths more often to burp after a Michelob than to let out their feelings. Breeding tells. Women never heard members of their sex described as the strong, silent type or grew up with role models like Gary Cooper, who made a simple "yup" make audiences say yes at the box office. So, when men do talk, women have to listen—and then not believe half of what they hear. The following helps you decide which half.

MAN'S STATEMENT	REAL TALK
I buy *Playboy* to read the articles.	*I just cut out the pictures to hang on my wall.*
I need some time.	*With you I feel as if I'm doing time.*
I think we should get to know each other better too.	*And what better way than in the biblical sense.*

MAN'S STATEMENT	REAL TALK
I told you I didn't want to get serious.	*At least give me credit for not lying.*
Did you come?	*I hope so because I'm out of here.*
I'm not ready to be tied down.	*To me, baby, that's really S&M.*
I don't want a woman who's a *complete* bimbo.	*Looking like one is enough for me.*
What's a little cellulite?	*That a little liposuction won't cure.*
A marriage certificate is only a piece of paper.	*So is a warrant for my arrest.*
Beauty is only skin deep.	*But who wants to look at a girl's intestines?*
I don't see any reason to jump into anything.	*Except bed.*
You're right—sex isn't everything.	*It's just the thing we don't have enough of.*

MAN'S STATEMENT	REAL TALK
It just happened.	*After I bought her a drink, got her number, called, wined and dined her, took her to a motel . . . it finally just happened.*
Man is not a monogamous animal.	*We're just animals.*
I like a woman with a good head on her shoulders.	*So she can get a good job and foot the bills.*
I believe in until death do us part.	*That's why I'd feel like killing myself if I got married.*
So what if you're small-busted—more than a handful is wasted.	*On the hand maybe—but not the eyes, baby.*
She has a good sense of humor.	*She has the good sense to laugh at my jokes.*
Let's lie down in the bedroom and watch TV.	*You get the picture.*

MAN'S STATEMENT	REAL TALK
I'll call you.	*Chances are you'll call me every name in the book before I do.*
Women can have it all.	*I'll just take the half that doesn't include waxy yellow build-up and ring around the collar.*
I like a woman who's smart.	*Enough to tell me I am.*
Love is blind.	*But, unfortunately, marriage gives you microscopic vision.*

CHAPTER THREE ☙☙☙

How the World Really Works

Generally—as much as one can generalize without some nitpicker pointing out all the exceptions—there are two types of jobs: the underrated ones you are underpaid to do and the overrated ones you have to overpay people to do for you. Of course, to afford the so-called services of others such as the contractor who will screw you (that's not a pun; that's Real Talk), the lawn care people who don't care, you probably have to—as the song and the unemployment office say—get a job. So, first the search.

Declassified Information: What the Want Ads Really Want

The want ads are not what they're written up to be. You can't just read them, you have to read into them. And to do that, you have to apply yourself. The following supplement should help with the preliminary job—psyching out the classifieds.

CLASSIFIED AD	REAL TALK
Must work well under pressure.	*Last three predecessors had nervous breakdowns.*
Free training.	*Nobody would spend their own money to learn how to do this job.*
Must have own car.	*To run into the ground on our behalf.*
Flexible hours.	*You'll never know what hour of the day or night we'll need you.*
Send salary history.	*So we don't offer more than we have to.*
Work at home.	*We can't afford office space for you.*
Room for advancement.	*You can't sink any lower here.*

CLASSIFIED AD	REAL TALK
No experience necessary.	*If you had experience, it wouldn't be necessary for you to take this crummy job.*
Right hand to top executive.	*Think about everything his right hand does.*
Team work.	*You're on the assembly line.*
A career with a future.	*Doesn't offer much at present.*
Fast-paced atmosphere.	*Burn out quickly.*
Profit sharing.	*The company isn't showing a profit.*
Earn huge commissions.	*Get no salary.*
Diversified duties.	*You do everything.*
Highly visible position in company.	*Receptionist.*
Must be highly motivated.	*To stoop to do this work.*

CLASSIFIED AD	REAL TALK
Must be self-starter.	*Nobody to show you what to do.*
Convenient to all public transportation.	*In dangerous, downtown area.*
Must make good impression in front office.	*Must have impressive front.*
Must be in great shape.	*And not afraid to show it.*
Rub elbows with celebrities.	*Massage their egos . . . or whatever else needs massaging.*
Unlimited income stuffing envelopes at home.	*No limit to the number of people who tell us to take this job and shove it.*

The Job Interview: Looking at It from a Different Point of View

Honesty may be the best policy in a job interview—if you don't care about getting the job. Of course, this doesn't mean faking being a brain surgeon when the only place you learned to cut anything was at Wilfred Beauty Academy. Rather this refers more to putting your best foot forward without announcing you have a hole in your sock. Not that interviewees are the only ones who may play it less than straight. "An office with a view," for example, can turn out to be a view of an alley with garbage cans. Euphemisms like the following—and the use of euphemism here is itself a euphemism—are made to work overtime in a few departments.

The Firing Lines

Getting fired is not the worst thing that can happen. Admitting it in a job interview is. So, failure is the father of invention in this instance. (Mothers have gotten enough bad raps.) The following stock phrases indicate one has been canned, without opening up the proverbial can of worms.

EXPLANATION	REAL TALK
There were budget cuts.	*I'm what was cut from the budget.*
There was a decision to cut down on overhead.	*My supervisor decided I was over my head.*
There was a major policy change.	*Their policy was to keep only people who make a contribution.*
I felt I deserved time off to travel.	*Especially to recuperate from the trauma of being let go.*
My entire department was no longer necessary.	*Once they made me head of the department.*
I feel a career change is in order.	*Since the last three companies that let me go felt that way.*
They reduced the size of my group.	*By one.*
They eliminated my function in the office.	*After they saw I couldn't function.*
There was the usual cutback.	*I'm the one that got the ax as usual.*

EXPLANATION	REAL TALK
I decided to go back to school.	*When I was told not to come back to work.*
My job was done away with.	*Because I wasn't doing my job.*
There was a reorganization.	*They decided I had nothing to offer the organization.*
The firm is planning to relocate.	*Employees like me to other companies.*
They concluded certain job categories were dispensable.	*They concluded I was in the dispensable category.*
I thought being a househusband would be an interesting alternative.	*To just saying I couldn't get a job.*
I believed a woman's place was in the home.	*After I was told there was no place for me in the office.*
I decided it was time to smell the roses.	*Since my company thought it was time to send me out to pasture.*

What a Job Interviewer Is Truly Telling You

Job interviewers tend to bend the truth in only three situations: (1) when they are trying to get you to take the job; (2) when they are making up their minds whether you're the one for the job; and (3) when they've decided they don't want you for the job. In short: at any time. The following put-ons are based upon input from seasoned job seekers ("who have the scars to prove it"). As one interviewee who got stabbed in the back—by a headhunter—warned about interviews, "Just act as if you're negotiating an arms treaty, 'Trust but verify.' "

Take My Offer, Please

A Wall Street executive upon being pressed to sign with a firm was promised—in writing—a million dollar bonus "if he delivered." (This was b.c.—before the crash.) Five years later the case is just going to court to get the company "to deliver." The outcome may not be known yet, but the smaller come-ons below are all too familiar.

COMPANY COME-ON	REAL TALK
You'll have your own secretary, of course.	*You'll share with four other executives as a matter of course.*

COMPANY COME-ON	REAL TALK
Even in bad times, we remember our employees at Christmas.	*We're talking turkey— literally.*
The firm hopes to move to a more scenic location.	*One-half mile from the president's house, 50 miles from yours.*
We like to reward our employees with merit increases.	*But we usually don't unless they threaten to leave.*
We plan on redoing your office some time soon.	*Count on making do with your office for some time.*
We think of our company as one big family.	*We're big on making your family come to a lot of company events.*
You're free to take your vacation the week of Fourth of July, Labor Day . . . or anytime.	*If you can convince all the other people with more seniority not to take it at that time.*

COMPANY COME-ON	REAL TALK
We like to promote from the inside.	*Because we have a hard time recruiting from the outside.*
We give continuous cost-of-living increases.	*Yeah, the cost of living in Calcutta.*

Never Let Them See You Sweat

If you weren't in the hot seat when going for a job, Madison Avenue wouldn't spend millions to sell you a deodorant on the premise, "Never let them see you sweat." Not to get gross, but does anybody say a word about the interviewer's perspiration problems? No. Indeed, if interviewers get hot under the collar or wherever, they're free to take off their jackets and roll up their shirt sleeves. Many how-to books on job hunting advise the industrious applicant to follow suit—which is reason enough to wear one.

So, you're the guy (even if you're a gal, face it, you're one of the boys now) who has to play it cool—and come out of that interview smelling like a rose. What makes this tricky is sniffing out what interviewers really do have up their sleeves.

INTERVIEWER'S COMMENT	REAL TALK
What is your greatest weakness?	*Being an incurable workaholic rates a 10; possibly needing a few days off for shock treatments now and then is less than zero.*
I see here you have three children.	*A picture of them on your desk is all we'd like to see of them here.*
Would you object to taking a drug test?	*Just say no.*
Twenty years is certainly a long time to have stayed in one position.	*A robot would have gotten itself promoted by now.*
How does your spouse feel about you getting a job in a different city?	*If not raring for you to go, then get a different job or spouse, whichever you prefer.*

INTERVIEWER'S COMMENT	REAL TALK
Yes, you've mentioned the Regional Marketing Plan you wrote as one of your qualifications for the job.	*As many times as Dan Quayle mentioned he authored the Job Training Program—but again do you have any other qualifications for the job?*
You seem to have a lot of interesting hobbies.	*For someone supposedly interested in your career.*
It's quite unusual for someone in your field to have gotten two master's degrees *and* a Ph.D.	*It's quite stupid for someone in your field to waste that much time in school.*
Now, are you sure you have *no* questions or *anything* to add to what's on your résumé?	*For heaven's sake, say something—you're not applying for Vanna White's job.*
I guess that exhausts all the questions *you* have.	*Give it a rest, already. I'm starting to feel like a guest on a Barbara Walters special.*

INTERVIEWER'S COMMENT	REAL TALK
So, what made you interested in selling pickles?	*You were born to pitch pickles or you're in one.*
You understand even though you'll be an administrative assistant, there will be some typing and filing.	*You understand a secretary by any other name is a secretary.*
I wouldn't ask anybody who worked for me to do anything I wouldn't do myself.	*I just wouldn't ask for them to get paid anything near what I get paid myself.*
Hmn, it's listed here that you're, uh, separated—not that that situation has anything to do with this job, mind you.	*But inquiring minds want to know.*

The Lowdown on Why You Didn't Get That Job

You can bet your unemployment check you won't be told by a prospective employer that you were turned down for a job because you're fat, female, forty, look like a before-ad for an acne commercial, or wear a ring in your nose. They will just discuss this behind your back. Interviewers admitted (when threatened by nonstop pestering by the author) they don't take pains to explain the reason for rejection because "what's in it for us?" But there could be something for you. To know the dirt on why you struck out could help you strike paydirt next go-round. Hence, this short and sour guide (there's no need to wallow here) to put-ons behind the brush-offs:

BRUSH-OFF	REAL TALK

Oldies, But Baddies

You're overqualified.

1. *You're overage.*
2. *Whatever your age, you're over the hill.*
3. *You're over our pay scale.*

BRUSH-OFF	REAL TALK
	4. *You'd be over my head—and maybe after my job.*
	5. *You'd be out of here, as soon as you can get another job.*
	6. *It's time to get this interview over with— and this is a time-honored way to do it.*
We decided to hire from the inside.	*After we saw you're what's on the outside.*
We don't need someone with this much experience.	*From our experience we don't need to pay someone this much.*
We've decided to put a freeze on hiring.	*You leave us cold.*
Our management team is in place.	*There's no place for you in our management.*
Yes, you can leave your résumé in case anything opens up.	*The only thing that will open up is the garbage can where we toss the résumé.*

Experienced in Marketing

BRUSH-OFF	REAL TALK

Ladies' Day Specials

We wanted someone experienced in marketing.

Marketing in the A&P is not what we had in mind.

Your volunteer work is quite impressive.

To the Junior League maybe—but not to our senior management.

We were looking for someone who had more extensive accomplishments.

Winning the Pillsbury Bake-off is not one of them.

For New Women Only (Or Heads, Not Tails)

We were looking for someone who can come up with a lot of new ideas.

Not just give men the same old ones.

NQOK (Not Quite Our Kind)

We generally like to recruit *our* people right out of school.

1. You're not from the right school.

BRUSH-OFF	REAL TALK
	2. And even if you are, you should have been there 20 years ago.
We were looking for someone with more of a track record.	*Not someone who looks like he has a record.*

For Appearance' Sake Only

BRUSH-OFF	REAL TALK
We want someone who has had heavy front office experience.	*We don't want someone in the front office who's heavy.*
We were looking for someone who is used to dealing with our type of clientele.	Our *clientele is used to dealing with the Brooks— not the Blues—Brothers type. Clean up your act.*

How Not to Toot Your Horn

BRUSH-OFF	REAL TALK
Well, uh, I suppose technically speaking, you *could* say you've been in the automobile business as long as Lee Iacocca.	*Look, bub, I know Lee Iacocca. I worked for Lee Iacocca . . . You're no Lee Iacocca.*

BRUSH-OFF	REAL TALK

Where We're Coming From

We wouldn't want the expense of relocating you from L.A.

Like, you know, your Val girl accent wouldn't be a credit to us, okay? Okay.

We wouldn't want the expense of relocating you from N.Y.

Those dese, dems, and dose have got to go.

Oh, Grow Up, First

We wanted someone who has worked in a fast-paced environment.

Not someone who's only worked in a fast-food restaurant.

CHAPTER FOUR ∽∽∽∽

Hitting Home

There's no place like home. And it'll seem as if there's no home you can afford if you're looking in today's unreal real estate market. But luckily one day you're likely to pass the dream-on stage. Then you'll have just the nightmare of fixing and keeping up your dream house. This guide tries to give you shelter; and while it may not get you in *House Beautiful*, it should keep you from winding up in a rest home.

Padded Ads for Pads

Whether you have a real estate pro in tow or go it alone, don't leave to look for a home without this addendum to the ads. It might steer you away from some roads that shouldn't be taken—and stop you from being taken in.

REAL ESTATE AD	REAL TALK

Houses for Sale

REAL ESTATE AD	REAL TALK
Place has potential.	*For a nervous breakdown, if you ever try to fix the place up.*
Below market price.	*Below par.*
Large staff quarters.	*Needs a large staff to keep it up.*
House needs updating.	*Don't set a date for the housewarming.*
A real dollhouse.	*Perfect for Barbie and Ken—not real people.*
From a bygone era.	*The house is a goner.*
Great place to raise children.	*And depress sophisticated adults.*
Built with lots of love by owner.	*Owner would love to sell for lots of money.*
One-of-a-kind lot.	*No two could have such an irregular shape.*

REAL ESTATE AD	REAL TALK
Adjoining open land.	*For now—deal being closed to build condos on land.*
Perfect starter house.	*You wouldn't want to end up here.*

Vacation Homes

REAL ESTATE AD	REAL TALK
Oceanfront.	*Front of house has occasionally gone in ocean.*
On the water.	*And under it during storms.*
Live by the sea.	*May have to live on sushi if house goes out to sea.*
Mountainside house.	*House may fall down side of mountain during mud slide.*
Breathtaking view from highest point.	*We're always out of breath—that's the point.*
Get away from it all.	*All the conveniences are far away.*
Back-to-nature setting.	*Get set for animals to creep in back door.*

REAL ESTATE AD	REAL TALK
Originally a barn.	*The smell will tell.*

Apts./Co-ops/Condos

Superintendent on premises.	*And on Jack Daniels.*
Walk to restaurants.	*Especially the Chinese one a flight below you.*
No board approval needed for this building.	*You won't approve of the people in this building.*
Mint condition.	*You'll need a mint to buy it.*
Customized to owner's unique taste.	*And what a waste— nobody else can get accustomed to mirrored ceilings and purple carpeting.*
Within easy reach of all entertainment.	*Noise from all-night disco will reach your bedroom window.*
Building going co-op.	*Tenants going crazy.*

REAL ESTATE AD	REAL TALK
Has kitchenette.	*Fit for a Smurfette.*
One block to subway.	*Noise travels.*
Convenient to all stores.	*You'll be inconvenienced by crowds that shop at them.*
Unique triplex.	*Unique way to triple exercise.*
The security is tight.	*So is the doorman.*
Old-world style concierge on premises.	*Old man in lobby who can't understand English will be taking your messages.*
Buy now and get in on ground floor.	*Buy now so we get the money to break ground for project.*

How They Try to Fix You

After you've gone for broke for a place to live, one thing you can count on like clockwork—if the clock's still working—is that something will break the minute you move in. Moreover, as soon as one item goes kaput, one right after another will surely follow on cue. Given this disorder of things, some object of your affection will always need a helping handyman. Then, there is the keeping up with the high-tech factor. One can't expect a genuine Colonial home to have been built with a hot tub—or even a simple burglar alarm. The owners probably just listened for Paul Revere. That's where the trouble comes in. The reputations of repairmen and workmen of all types have fallen into disrepair. Here are some ways, if left to their own devices, they will fix *you*.

STATEMENT	REAL TALK
Someone will be there between nine and five.	*That someone may just be you waiting for us to come.*
The spray our exterminators use isn't harmful to your health.	*Or to your roaches—that's why they're still in your kitchen.*
You won't smell this paint.	*If you move to a hotel for a while.*

STATEMENT	REAL TALK
We don't remove paint, lady.	*We just drop it on the floor—you have to get it off.*
Our back-to-nature swimming pools blend in with your natural setting.	*If you live in Tahiti—not Teaneck, New Jersey.*
The job should take six weeks.	*But they won't be consecutive ones.*
We use no chemicals on your shrubs.	*And we don't keep off the bugs.*
We can turn a wreck into a palace.	*For a king's ransom.*
I know construction because I've been in it a long time.	*There's no way to short-change you I haven't learned.*
We can put in your swimming pool by summer.	*If you can put up with a hole in your yard fall, winter, and spring.*

STATEMENT	REAL TALK
This will keep your heating bills down.	*What you save will be a small fraction of our insulation bill.*
The right shrubbery can turn your house into an estate.	*A forest big enough to hide that it's a tract house.*
This new heating system will pay for itself.	*But I won't wait for it to pay for my services.*
Installation is free.	*It's built into the cost of the product.*
We remove walls.	*You pick up the debris.*
Same-day service.	*We may show up the same day we say.*
We can add a wing.	*But it may take a year off your life.*
Well, that bill includes overtime.	*That we had to put in because we didn't work the regularly scheduled times.*

Why You May Want to Finish Off the Decorator

The right decorator can do wonders, but the wrong one can make you wonder if something's wrong with you for using him or her. Not that you're going to live together. But you do have to live with how this person puts your place together. Worse, if you select a strictly top-drawer decorator you may have to live with a bunch of put-downs as well. In this respect—or rather disrespect—you can tell as much from tone and shading as words. The following comments were construed as digs by clients who got the urge to deck their decorators—if not finish them off.

DECORATOR'S DIG	REAL TALK
Well, it's a matter of taste.	*And obviously you don't have any.*
There's nothing like letting go of the past.	*Especially since there's nothing here but your past mistakes.*
Pictures of ancestors are usually a must in a house.	*But in your house we must use someone else's ancestors.*

DECORATOR'S DIG	REAL TALK
Of course, we can use some of what you have.	*Yeah, the lightbulbs and plumbing pipes.*
Well, uh, yes, your *faux* French Provincial furniture is fine.	*For the Salvation Army.*
Your husband's sure he really needs that vinyl recliner?	*Are you sure you really need that husband?*
Well, your present living room wouldn't fit on "Lifestyles of the Rich and Famous" . . . ha, ha, ha.	*It's more along the lines of "Lifestyles of the Poor and Unknown."*
I suppose *some* people like track lighting.	*People from the wrong side of the tracks.*
Plus you're doing a good deed by giving this all away.	*You should get on your knees and thank Goodwill for taking it away.*
I could make this a drop-dead living room.	*What you'll drop dead from is the price.*

DECORATOR'S DIG	REAL TALK
So, *this* is what you call the guest room.	*It's a wonder your guests don't call Ramada Inn.*
You'll see, a library can even give *you* hours of pleasure.	*If you keep it well stocked with brandy.*
A room says so much about you.	*This room is saying loud, terrible things about you.*
It's not how your guests will sit on backless chairs.	*It's how my designs will sit with Architectural Digest.*

Movers: They Can Pile It On

If upkeep is a headache, packing it in and moving on is a migraine. Moreover, movers don't spell relief. It's been estimated the average American moves five times, and that can seem like five times too many—unless you're married to one of the Santini Brothers. The following may not make the going smooth, but it should help you keep your hired hands on the level.

MOVER'S STATEMENT	REAL TALK
Everything breakable will be marked "Fragile."	*Of course, not every one of our boys can read.*

MOVER'S STATEMENT	REAL TALK
We only set the painting down for a second in the lobby, lady.	*Is it our fault it only takes a second for a painting to get stolen from your lobby, lady?*
Don't worry, our men are bonded.	*They just look like they're out on bail.*
We did the best we could with the china.	*Those are the breaks.*
All the upholstered pieces are specially covered.	*We can't help it if the covers aren't especially clean.*
We'll just take the desk apart, that's all.	*That is all—nobody's saying we can put it back together again.*
We've moved a lot of antiques.	*And a lot of the furniture we move just looks antique when we're finished with it.*
We try to make your load lighter.	*And when we're done— you'll see it will be.*

MOVER'S STATEMENT	REAL TALK
We give free estimates.	*But we don't give promises to stick to them.*
We're the friendly moving company.	*Our movers will get so friendly you'll think you're entertaining company.*
The fee for the job doesn't count the tips to the men.	*Tip: Don't count on the men doing the job if you don't tip.*
It pays to take the time beforehand to make an inventory of what's being moved.	*It'll save you time afterward figuring out what didn't survive the move.*
We can store your belongings.	*Hopefully, you'll be able to restore them.*

CHAPTER FIVE

A Real Buy: Shopping, American Style

If you were born to shop, you can thank your lucky stripes and stars you were Born in the USA. (You can also thank Bruce Springsteen for that line.) Love may make the world go round, but in America, it's the revolving charge. And never more so than in these Deficit Decades. Shopping malls are now the center of our Mainless Street suburban universe and it is here that we come of age by undergoing the rite of passage—learning the value of the credit card. TV's "Family Ties" star, Mallory (Justine Bateman) Keaton, when asked in philosophy class to prove her existence, summed up a generation with, "I shop, therefore I am."

But in a nation dedicated to the building and selling of a

better mousetrap and any other contraption people will snap up, there are a lot of catches. And that's where this consumer guide should come in handy. It delivers some Real Talk to make you a sharper, albeit curmudgeonlike shopper—which, for my money, beats being a sucker who's bilked every minute.

Off to a Bad Start

USED CAR: *What the person who knows it best has no use for.*

Congratulations! If you are buying a used car, you're off to a bad start—and it's a smart move to deal with the worst first. Used car salesmen, as a lot, are in a crass by themselves, so to speak. However, if this is the route you want to go, the checklist mapped out below will signal you to what's ahead and get you in gear to shop among the sharks.

MECHANICALLY SPEAKING	REAL TALK
Rebuilt engine.	*After it fell apart.*
New paint job.	*Hot car.*
Kept in garage.	*Needed constant repairs.*

MECHANICALLY SPEAKING	REAL TALK
Original owner.	*Willard Scott just celebrated the owner's 100th birthday on "The Today Show."*
Needs tune-up.	*If you'd like to be able to hear the radio rather than that loud, nonstop hum.*
Low mileage.	*High chance the odometer has been tampered with.*
Some bodywork needed.	*We're talking major metal meltdown here.*
Test drive.	*Allowing you to drive a car a few miles to see if it will last thousands. Get real.*
Just arrived on the lot.	*Just retrieved from the junk yard.*
Take over payments.	*Before finance company takes over car.*
Needs minor repairs.	*Weekly.*
Good body.	*At least you can sell it for scrap.*

Have We Got a Deal for You

Whatever you buy, you often don't get what you bargained
for because you're being sold a bill of goods as part of the
package. The following claims may not put companies to
shame, but they should put you on the alert.

CLAIM	REAL TALK
Free in-home service guarantee.	*A guarantee the product can never be serviced at home.*
Accessories are not included.	*But are essential to operate the machine.*
Stubborn stains will disappear.	*So will your fabric.*
A child could operate this product.	*A child prodigy.*
Learn to speak French in three weeks.	*To someone else who has been speaking French for only three weeks.*
Self-cleaning oven.	*You'll wind up cleaning it yourself.*

CLAIM	REAL TALK
Once in a lifetime offer.	*Nobody would be fool enough to fall for it twice.*
Our customers swear by this product.	*And at our customer representatives.*
Tamper-proof cap.	*Only the criminally insane can open it.*
Specially waterproofed.	*Especially if you don't go near the water.*
Wash and wear.	*Wash and wear it wrinkled.*
Easily assembled.	*By those with advanced degrees on our engineering staff.*
Batteries included.	*And dead upon arrival.*
We carry the latest movies on video.	*Just not on the days you want them.*
Free consultation.	*We don't charge for the sales pitch.*
Dry cleaning recommended.	*If you want to wear this more than once.*

CLAIM	REAL TALK
Instant check-out line.	*It fills up the instant you try to get in it.*
Countless cures.	*No one has counted them.*
This VCR has more functions than any model ever.	*You won't be able to get the VCR to function in more ways than ever.*
Our sales representative will be in your neighborhood tomorrow.	*If we can talk you into an appointment today.*
Marked down from regular price.	*No one would pay the regular price.*
No sales representative will call on you.	*They'll just hound you by mail and phone.*
Offer available for a limited time only.	*Offer will not be available by the time you can take us up on it.*
Only your hairdresser will know for sure.	*But everybody else will be able to guess, for sure.*
Prices are subject to change.	*Prices will go up.*

On Their Terms

SALES FORCE: *People employed by a store to try to force you to buy something.*

A salesman or woman does lend a personal touch to shopping, as long as you remember that this is a person hired to put the touch on you. If they were there to help you, they would be called helpers. What helps is to keep this planted in mind. Otherwise, you may find yourself planted in a return/exchange line (the point of no return in many stores), because when you got home—and out from under the influence of a saleswoman who could give Philip Roth's mother guilt lessons—you realized the only thing the color puce does for you is to make you puke. No, seeing it in a different light did not make the slightest shade of difference. The following will prepare you for meeting salespeople on their terms.

SALES TALK	REAL TALK
Oh, those shoes will give.	*You a lot of aches and pains.*
May I help you?	*Spend your money.*

SALES TALK	**REAL TALK**
This dress runs big, so I gave you the next smaller size.	*We're out of your size.*
This dress runs small, so I gave you the next larger size.	*We're out of your size.*
This is *the* color this year.	*Mauve is the only color we have left as no one is buying it this year.*
Both dresses look great.	*It would be great if you bought both dresses.*
Young girls are wearing three-inch heels this year.	*If you're not willing to kill your feet too, you're an old bag.*
High heels do so much for your legs.	*Your legs need so much done for them.*
You just have to break them in first.	*You'll break your neck first.*
You'll feel fine once you wear them awhile.	*I'll feel fine once you wear them awhile because then you can't return them.*

SALES TALK	REAL TALK
Will that be all?	*Is that all you have the gall to buy after I gave you the best hours of my day?*
Thank you, come again.	*Spend again.*

Shopping Catalogs: Not What the Customer Ordered

In this modern age of you-name-it, we-deliver-it, slam-bam, thank-you, ma'am, you don't have to knock yourself out to shop. You can turn to catalogs. They carry it all—from French ticklers to tofu, plus items more normal people like, thank goodness. Of course, when your order arrives you may not know what's in store for you, because you were too lazy to go to one. Serves you right is the unofficial catalog motto. For example, that itty-bitty print you couldn't read under the picture may have said, "Actual size of product not shown." Or your 20-piece set of china may come in 46 pieces—at no extra charge, mind you.

But who can give up all this convenience—or stop those unsolicited catalogs that crush the important letters in your mailbox? So, for those who can't get off the mail order junket, here's a little ad lib to make you a cagier catalog shopper before you place your order—make that place your bet.

Not What the Customer Ordered

CATALOG COME-ON	REAL TALK
You've never seen anything like these precious jewels.	*Without a magnifying glass.*
Please give second choice for color.	*We won't have your first.*
Money refunded promptly with no questions asked.	*Except those that take up two sides of the exchange form.*
Packed in ice.	*Will arrive in water.*
Fits any size.	*But yours.*
Orders taken 24 hours a day.	*By a computer that can't possibly tell you if the sweater you want runs large, idiot.*
Delivered fresh upon arrival.	*At our place—not yours.*
Call our toll-free number.	*For a busy signal.*
We ship all orders within 14 days unless you're notified otherwise.	*Wise up, you'll be notified otherwise.*

CATALOG COME-ON	REAL TALK
Fruit picked ripe from the vine.	*Fruit will be so rotten you won't want to pick it up from the crate.*
Complete convenient order blank.	*Designed for our computer's convenience, not yours.*
Ham delivered fresh from Old Virginia.	*To our old warehouse in Brooklyn.*
Natural-looking flowers.	*But, naturally, anybody who looks at them can see they're artificial.*
We use no preservatives.	*The product will not be preserved during shipping.*
Photograph of product is enlarged to show exquisite details.	*The detail we're leaving out here is the photograph is nothing like the product.*
We occasionally make our customers' names available to selected companies.	*Congratulations—you have just been selected to be on every junk mail list in the USA.*

CHAPTER SIX

And the Real Talk Goes On...

Real Talk is where you can find it—and that can be anywhere. The following quick mix shows some other directions where you have to keep your antenna up.

Political Realities: Or Why Voters Can't Win

When a politician says something publicly, voters have to separate the rhetoric from the real. The following is a sampling of little white lies as well as big White House ones. But there's no favoritism here because both parties talk out of both sides of their mouths.

POLITICIAN'S STATEMENT	REAL TALK
Watch closely America . . . my running mate is going to make a great Vice-President.	*You'll have to watch closely—Howard Hughes was seen more in public than this guy will be.*
I chose my running mate because of what he could bring to the ticket.	*All those electoral votes from that big state of his that's too dumb to give them to me otherwise.*
As President I will not propose new programs that increase taxes.	*The Congress will do that for me.*

POLITICIAN'S STATEMENT	REAL TALK
I see a thousand points of light.	*And every time I do I think I might be having a stroke.*
I did have a plan to clean up the toxic waste in Boston Harbor.	*I figured we could ship it to New Jersey because they had so much they wouldn't notice a little more anyway.*
I don't believe in negative campaigns.	*Because my opponent is better at saying negative things about me than we are about him, damn it.*
My main goal is to create good-paying jobs in this country.	*Starting with ones for myself and my cronies.*
I have a vision for this country.	*I keep seeing myself in the Oval Office.*
I'm behind my choice for Vice-President 1,000%.	*Unless he causes me to be too far behind in the polls.*

POLITICIAN'S STATEMENT	REAL TALK
My running mate and I do disagree, but we agree on the fundamental issues.	*Primarily, that we should be in power.*
We lost the election, but now it's time to pull together.	*Against that sleazeball, to make him look like the loser he is.*
I've put the matter of infidelity behind me.	*This f------ infidelity thing is making me fall behind.*
I'm not some Tammy Wynette standing behind my man.	*I'm too busy pushing him toward the White House.*
The voters want to get on to the important issues and get off my personal life.	*Get off my back.*
I didn't inhale.	*Yeah—and I pulled out too.*
I may not be perfect, but I'm honest.	*To be perfectly honest, that's why some say I can't win.*

Phoniness on the Phone

The telephone has been instrumental in stretching the truth because it's harder to get somebody's number when you're not talking person-to-person. TV ads have promoted "Relaxation," "Comfort," "Get Rid of the Guilt," and a variety of feel-good calls. But at the other end of the line, there are calls with a phoney ring to them that it pays to be plugged into.

THE LINE	REAL TALK

The Saved by the Bell Call

Oh, I have to go, there's somebody at my door.	*Thank God. I've never been so glad to see a Jehovah's Witness in my life.*

The Getting Off the Hook Call

Oh, hi, I was going to call you.	*Yeah, right after I did my taxes and got my apartment painted.*

The I'm Out of Here Call

Who's calling? . . . Oh, she's not in.	*To you.*

THE LINE	REAL TALK

The Cliché Call

Have a nice day.

Even though I've just done my best to ruin it.

The Busy Signal

Gee, listen, you caught me at a bad time—I have to, uh, get ready to go to the doctor's.

Well, listening to your troubles does make me sick.

The Who's on First Call

This is Mr. Big's secretary. If you put on Mr. Not-As-Big-In-Our-Book, Mr. Big will talk to him now.

He who comes on the line himself first, ranks last.

The Get Lost Call

Oh, hi, I was going to get back to you, but I lost your number.

Because what did I have to gain from keeping it?

THE LINE	REAL TALK

The Power Call

This is his secretary. I'm returning your call to let you know . . .

First off, that he's too important to return a call personally to you.

The Do You Hold Any Weight Call

Oh, that's my call-waiting. Can you hold? I'll just be a minute.

Unless the other person holds more weight than you.

The You Can't Chew Me Out Call

I returned your call yesterday about noon.

When I knew you'd be out to lunch and I wouldn't have to chew the fat with you.

The People Who Need People Call

Love ya, baby. My people will be in touch with your people.

People who have mere people to do their calling are People.

THE LINE	REAL TALK

The Cellular Solution

Oh, you were in the Rolls— I must have just tried the Porsche and the Jag.	*That's rich.**

The Fast Track Call

With my schedule, it's never a good time to talk.	*To you—to someone who would put me in the Cellular Solution class, well, that's another story.*

Answering Machines: The Unspoken Message

Did you ever get a message on an answering machine that said, "Hi, I'm in right now screening my calls. Speak at the beep. If I want to talk to you, I'll pick up. Otherwise, buzz off." Probably not, as that would be too rude for words. But people do answer the phone all the time *after* a sneak preview of the call. Except those who pick up mid-message are apt to opt for crudeness over rudeness (or at least make uncalled for references to bodily functions), which is why you're likely to hear, "Oh, I was in the bathroom . . ." In-

* Eat your heart out—this was really overheard in Beverly Hills.

deed, this is said so often, one would think there's been a run on Kaopectate since the advent of the answering machine—if one didn't know this whole routine was a crock. Here are some other ways people mask that they've been secretly deciding if you pass the screening test.

EXCUSE	REAL TALK
1. Hi, I was in the shower. (This cleans up the bathroom act—but suggestively. So, not suggested for a member of opposite sex you wouldn't want to shower with.)	*I'm screening my calls.*
2. I was running the vacuum and didn't hear the phone. (But who could miss your big mouth? Nice compliment.)	*I'm screening my calls.*
3. I forgot my machine was on. (Only valid for those of President Reagan's age—or temperament.)	*I'm screening my calls.*

EXCUSE	REAL TALK
4. I was in the kitchen cooking. (Unless you're Julia Child, cool it. What do you take people for? This is the take-out generation.)	*I'm screening my calls.*
5. Oh, hi, I was upstairs and just ran down. (Even if heavy breathing is heard, people will doubt running is what it's from.)	*I'm screening my calls.*
6. Oh, I was taking a nap. (Do you really want to raise the question of why you need one?)	*I'm screening my calls.*
7. I just walked in the door, would you believe it? (No.)	*I'm screening my calls.*

If You're Trying to Cheer Me Up, Why Do I Feel So Bad?

Under the wrong circumstances, remarks that seem well intended take on a different meaning. The following is just a sampling of ways a standard picker-upper can seem like a downer.

PICKER-UPPER	REAL TALK
There are plenty of other fish in the sea.	*Face it, he wasn't exactly Charlie the Tuna.*
Things could be worse.	*In Bangladesh maybe.*
You still *might* see him again.	*Yeah, you might spot Elvis too.*
The Lord giveth and the Lord taketh away.	*But rarely to and from the same people.*
Nobody can see you're missing a tooth.	*If you don't open your mouth.*
There's a man on every street corner.	*But, unfortunately, honey, in this city he's probably a mugger.*
Let's have lunch sometime.	*Yeah, in a next life.*

PICKER-UPPER	REAL TALK
Count your blessings.	*In your case, it'll only take a few minutes.*
I think it's interesting.	*You wouldn't be interested in what I really think.*
It's a free country.	*If you can afford it.*
Actually, I liked it better before.	*Actually, I don't like it now.*
Well, to be honest about it. . .	*I haven't been so far.*
Don't take it personally.	*Even though you're the person I'm sticking it to.*
I hope our little talk has helped you get over your cat passing on 10 years ago.	*Jeez, don't they have a 12-step program for that?*
At least you have your health.	*Now, get a life.*

CHAPTER SEVEN

Not the Last Word

Real Talk is a communication gap without end. So, to be a savvy communicator, the best way to finish this book is to begin a Real Talk notebook of your own—mental or written. If you don't stay plugged into Real Talk, you wind up out of it or holding the short end of the stick. But once you start using your "third ear" and putting what is said to the Real Talk Test, you'll be listening for success.

For the Record

SPEAKER   STATEMENT   REAL TALK

AFTERWORD: HERE'S ONE FOR THE (NEXT) BOOK

👄 If you pick up a bit of Real Talk that you would like to pass along, send it in for *Real Talk II*. It's a mumble-jumble jungle out there and those who want to know how to translate what is said into Real Talk need all the help they can get.

Send your Real Talk tip to:

Quill Ink/Maxim Publishing Corporation
177 Main Street
Suite 367
Dept. 2B
Fort Lee, NJ 07024

About the Author

Bret Ingham is a free-lance writer. Her work has appeared in *The New York Times*, *Harper's* magazine, the book *The Big Picture*, and other publications. Ms. Ingham lives in a suburb outside of New York City with her husband, who is an executive, a mischievous bichon frise puppy, who chewed up the best part of this manuscript, and a Real Talking cockatiel.

About the Illustrator

Roy McKie has illustrated and co-authored a number of best-selling humor books, including *Sailing* and *Gardening*.